The pages of this journaling tool represent the pattern I have developed for my own daily visits with God. The uses of the journal are as varied as the persons who choose to use it. Allow me to offer suggestions for those who may be new to journaling and personal devotions with the Lord

Journal

I enter the date and the weather. I use that as a place to begin my thoughts. From there I write out major events that have happened or will happen in the day. I may have a plan I am working on or something big I need to get done.

I record my Bible study time electronically and post them in a blog I call Daily Visits with God. You might elect to use this journal to record the Bible passage you read and the things you learned from the passage.

Prayer

You might use this section to write out a prayer list for the day or even write your prayer as you pray it. George Washington practiced that habit. His prayers during the Revolutionary War may be purchased still today and are a blessing to read. King David recorded many of his prayers in the Psalms. Sometimes I just write out a word to describe what I am praying about at the moment. The result is a prayer list "after the fact."

Blessings In

I like to keep a record of daily things I am grateful for. This might be phone calls, letters, emails and texts, etc. received. It might also just be a daily list of things you are thankful to God for. "I'm thankful I woke up. I'm thankful for my wife and kids, etc."

Blessings Out

This is a place to be purposeful about your faith. This is where I record visits, calls, or contacts with others I have made or plan to make. This is a great place to write out the names of people you want to witness to or be an encouragement to this day.

However you choose to use this journal my prayer is that it may be a blessing as you visit with God every day.

Marvin McKenzie

Journal

Prayer

Blessings In

Blessings Out

Journal

Prayer

Blessings In

Blessings Out

Journal

Prayer

Blessings In

Blessings Out

Journal

Prayer

Blessings In

Blessings Out

Journal

Prayer

Blessings
In

Blessings
Out

Journal

Prayer | Blessings In

Blessings Out

Journal

Prayer

Blessings In

Blessings Out

Journal

Prayer | Blessings In

Blessings Out

Journal

Prayer

Blessings In

Blessings Out

Journal

Prayer | Blessings In

Blessings Out

Journal

Prayer | Blessings In

Blessings Out

Journal

Prayer | Blessings In

Blessings Out

Journal

Prayer | Blessings In

| Blessings Out

Journal

Prayer | Blessings In

Blessings Out

Journal

Prayer | Blessings
In

Blessings
Out

Journal

Prayer | Blessings In

Blessings Out

Journal

Prayer | Blessings In

Blessings Out

Journal

Prayer | Blessings In

Blessings Out

Journal

Prayer

Blessings In

Blessings Out

Journal

Prayer | Blessings In

Blessings Out

Journal

Prayer | Blessings In

| Blessings Out

Journal

Prayer | Blessings In

Blessings Out

Journal

Prayer | Blessings In

Blessings Out

Journal

Prayer | Blessings In

Blessings Out

Journal

Prayer | Blessings In

Blessings Out

Journal

Prayer | Blessings In

Blessings Out

Journal

Prayer | Blessings In

Blessings Out

Journal

Prayer

Blessings In

Blessings Out

Journal

Prayer | Blessings In

Blessings Out

Journal

Prayer	Blessings In
	Blessings Out

Journal

Prayer | Blessings In

Blessings Out

Journal

Prayer

Blessings In

Blessings Out

Journal

Prayer | Blessings In

Blessings Out

Journal

Prayer | Blessings In

Blessings Out

Journal

Prayer | Blessings In

Blessings Out

Journal

Prayer

Blessings In

Blessings Out

Journal

Prayer | Blessings In

Blessings Out

Journal

Prayer | Blessings In

Blessings Out

Journal

Prayer

Blessings
In

Blessings
Out

Journal

Prayer

Blessings In

Blessings Out

Journal

Prayer | Blessings IN

| Blessings Out

Journal

Prayer | Blessings In

Blessings Out

Journal

Prayer | Blessings In

Blessings Out

Journal

Prayer | Blessings In

Blessings Out

Journal

Prayer

Blessings In

Blessings Out

Journal

Prayer | Blessings In

Blessings Out

Journal

Prayer | Blessings In

Blessings Out

Journal

Prayer | Blessings In

Blessings Out

Journal

Prayer	Blessings In
Blessings Out

Journal

Prayer | Blessings In
| Blessings Out

Journal

Prayer | Blessings In

Blessings Out

Journal

Prayer | Blessings In

Blessings Out

Journal

Prayer | Blessings
In

Blessings
Out

Journal

Prayer

Blessings
In

Blessings
Out

Journal

Prayer | Blessings In

Blessings Out

Journal

Prayer | Blessings In

Blessings Out

Journal

Prayer | Blessings In

Blessings Out

Journal

Prayer

Blessings
In

Blessings
Out

Journal

Prayer | Blessings In

Blessings Out

Journal

Prayer | Blessings In

Blessings Out

Journal

Prayer

Blessings In

Blessings Out

Journal

Prayer | Blessings In
 | Blessings Out

Journal

Prayer

Blessings In

Blessings Out

Journal

Prayer

Blessings In

Blessings Out

Journal

Prayer | Blessings In

Blessings Out

Journal

Prayer

Blessings In

Blessings Out

Journal

Prayer | Blessings In

Blessings Out

Journal

Prayer | Blessings
In

Blessings
Out

Journal

Prayer | Blessings In

| Blessings Out

Journal

Prayer

Blessings In

Blessings Out

Journal

Prayer | Blessings In

Blessings Out

Journal

Prayer | Blessings In

Blessings Out

Journal

Prayer

Blessings
In

Blessings
Out

Journal

Prayer | Blessings In

Blessings Out

Journal

Prayer | Blessings
In

| Blessings
Out

Journal

Prayer	Blessings In
	Blessings Out

Journal

Prayer | Blessings
In

Blessings
Out

Journal

Prayer | Blessings In

Blessings Out

Journal

Prayer | Blessings In

Blessings Out

Journal

Prayer

Blessings In

Blessings Out

Journal

Prayer | Blessings In

Blessings Out

Journal

Prayer | Blessings In

Blessings Out

Journal

Prayer

Blessings In

Blessings Out

Journal

Prayer | Blessings In

Blessings Out

Journal

Prayer | Blessings In
 |
 | Blessings Out

Journal

Prayer | Blessings In

Blessings Out

Journal

Prayer | Blessings In

Blessings Out

Journal

Prayer

Blessings
In

Blessings
Out

Journal

Prayer | Blessings In

Blessings Out

Journal

Prayer | Blessings In

Blessings Out

Journal

Prayer | Blessings In

Blessings Out

Journal

Prayer

Blessings In

Blessings Out

Journal

Prayer | Blessings In

Blessings Out

Journal

Prayer

Blessings In

Blessings Out

Journal

Prayer

Blessings
In

Blessings
Out

Journal

Prayer	Blessings In
	Blessings Out

Journal

Prayer | Blessings In

Blessings Out

Journal

Prayer | Blessings In

Blessings Out

Journal

Prayer

Blessings
In

Blessings
Out

Journal

Prayer

Blessings In

Blessings Out

Journal

Prayer | Blessings In

Blessings Out

Journal

Prayer | Blessings
In

Blessings
Out

Journal

Prayer | Blessings In

Blessings Out

Journal

Prayer

Blessings
In

Blessings
Out

Journal

Prayer | Blessings In
 |
 | Blessings Out

Journal

Prayer | Blessings In
 | Blessings Out

Journal

Prayer

Blessings In

Blessings Out

Journal

Prayer | Blessings In

Blessings Out

Journal

Prayer | Blessings In

Blessings Out

Journal

Prayer | Blessings In

Blessings Out

Journal

Prayer | Blessings In

Blessings Out

Journal

Prayer | Blessings In

Blessings Out

Journal

Prayer | Blessings In

Blessings Out

Journal

Prayer | Blessings In

Blessings Out

Journal

Prayer | Blessings In

Blessings Out

Journal

Prayer | Blessings In

Blessings Out

Journal

Prayer

Blessings In

Blessings Out

Journal

Prayer | Blessings In

Blessings Out

Journal

Prayer

Blessings In

Blessings Out

Journal

Prayer | Blessings In

Blessings Out

Journal

Prayer | Blessings In

Blessings Out

Journal

Prayer | Blessings In

Blessings Out

Journal

Prayer | Blessings In

Blessings Out

Journal

Prayer | Blessings In

Blessings Out

Journal

Prayer | Blessings In

Blessings Out

Journal

Prayer | Blessings In

Blessings Out

Journal

Prayer

Blessings In

Blessings Out

Journal

Prayer

Blessings In

Blessings Out

Journal

Prayer | Blessings
In

Blessings
Out

Journal

Prayer | Blessings In

Blessings Out

Journal

Prayer | Blessings In

Blessings Out

Journal

Prayer | Blessings In

Blessings Out

Journal

Prayer | Blessings In

Blessings Out

Journal

Prayer

Blessings In

Blessings Out

Journal

Prayer | Blessings In
 |
 | Blessings Out

Journal

Prayer | Blessings In

Blessings Out

Journal

Prayer | Blessings In
| Blessings Out

Journal

Prayer | Blessings In

Blessings Out

Journal

Prayer

Blessings
In

Blessings
Out

Journal

Prayer | Blessings In

Blessings Out

Journal

Prayer | Blessings In

Blessings Out

Journal

Prayer | Blessings In

Blessings Out

Journal

Prayer | Blessings In
        |
        | Blessings Out

Journal

Prayer | Blessings In

Blessings Out

Journal

Prayer | Blessings In
 | Blessings Out

Journal

Prayer

Blessings In

Blessings Out

Journal

Prayer

Blessings
In

Blessings
Out

Journal

Prayer | Blessings In
| Blessings Out

Journal

Prayer | Blessings In

Blessings Out

Journal

Prayer | Blessings In

Blessings Out

Journal

Prayer | Blessings In

Blessings Out

Journal

Prayer | Blessings In

Blessings Out

Journal

Prayer | Blessings In

Blessings Out

Journal

Prayer | Blessings In

Blessings Out

Journal

Prayer | Blessings In

Blessings Out

Journal

Prayer | Blessings In

Blessings Out

Journal

Prayer | Blessings
In

Blessings
Out

Journal

Prayer

Blessings In

Blessings Out

Journal

Prayer | Blessings
In

Blessings
Out

Journal

Prayer

Blessings
In

Blessings
Out

Journal

Prayer | Blessings In

Blessings Out

Journal

Prayer

Blessings In

Blessings Out

Journal

Prayer

Blessings In

Blessings Out

Journal

Prayer	Blessings In
	Blessings Out

Journal

Prayer

Blessings In

Blessings Out

Journal

Prayer | Blessings In

Blessings Out

Journal

Prayer

Blessings In

Blessings Out

Journal

Prayer | Blessings In

Blessings Out

Journal

Prayer | Blessings In
 | Blessings Out

Journal

Prayer | Blessings In

Blessings Out

Journal

Prayer

Blessings In

Blessings Out

Journal

Prayer | Blessings In

Blessings Out

Journal

Prayer | Blessings
In

Blessings
Out

Journal

Prayer | Blessings In

Blessings Out

Journal

Prayer | Blessings In

Blessings Out

Journal

Prayer | Blessings In

Blessings Out

Journal

Prayer | Blessings In

Blessings Out

Journal

Prayer | Blessings In

Blessings Out

Journal

Prayer | Blessings In

Blessings Out

Journal

Prayer | Blessings In

Blessings Out

Journal

Prayer | Blessings In

Blessings Out

Journal

Prayer | Blessings In

Blessings Out

Journal

Prayer | Blessings In

Blessings Out

Journal

Prayer | Blessings In

Blessings Out

Journal

Prayer | Blessings In

Blessings Out

Journal

Prayer | Blessings In

Blessings Out

Journal

Prayer | Blessings
 | In
 |
 | Blessings
 | Out

Journal

Prayer | Blessings In

Blessings Out

Journal

Prayer | Blessings In

Blessings Out

Journal

Prayer | Blessings In

Blessings Out

Journal

Prayer | Blessings In

Blessings Out

Journal

Prayer

Blessings In

Blessings Out

Journal

Prayer | Blessings
In

Blessings
Out

Journal

Prayer | Blessings In

Blessings Out

Journal

Prayer | Blessings
In

Blessings
Out

Journal

Prayer | Blessings In

Blessings Out

Journal

Prayer | Blessings
In

Blessings
Out

Journal

Prayer | Blessings In

Blessings Out

Journal

Prayer

Blessings In

Blessings Out

Journal

Prayer | Blessings In

Blessings Out

Journal

Prayer

Blessings
In

Blessings
Out

Journal

Prayer

Blessings
In

Blessings
Out

Journal

Prayer | Blessings In

Blessings Out

Journal

Prayer | Blessings In

Blessings Out

Journal

Prayer | Blessings In

Blessings Out

Journal

Prayer | Blessings In

Blessings Out

Journal

Prayer

Blessings
In

Blessings
Out

Journal

Prayer | Blessings In

Blessings Out

Journal

Prayer

Blessings
In

Blessings
Out

Journal

Prayer | Blessings In

Blessings Out

Journal

Prayer

Blessings
In

Blessings
Out

Journal

Prayer | Blessings In

Blessings Out

Journal

Prayer

Blessings
In

Blessings
Out

Journal

Prayer

Blessings In

Blessings Out

Journal

Prayer

Blessings
In

Blessings
Out

Journal

Prayer

Blessings In

Blessings Out

Journal

Prayer

Blessings In

Blessings Out

Journal

Prayer | Blessings In

Blessings Out

Journal

Prayer

Blessings
In

Blessings
Out

Journal

Prayer | Blessings In

Blessings Out

Journal

Prayer | Blessings In

Blessings Out

Journal

Prayer | Blessings In

Blessings Out

Journal

Prayer | Blessings In

Blessings Out

Journal

Prayer

Blessings
In

Blessings
Out

Journal

Prayer | Blessings In

Blessings Out

Journal

Prayer | Blessings In

Blessings Out

Journal

Prayer | Blessings In

Blessings Out

Journal

Prayer | Blessings In

Blessings Out

Journal

Prayer | Blessings
In

Blessings
Out

Journal

Prayer | Blessings In

Blessings Out

Journal

Prayer

Blessings
In

Blessings
Out

Journal

Prayer | Blessings In

Blessings Out

Journal

Prayer List

Blessings Received

Blessings to:

Journal

Prayer List	Blessings Received
	Blessings to:

Journal

Prayer List

Blessings Received

Blessings to:

Journal

Prayer | Blessings In

Blessings Out

Journal

Prayer | Blessings In

Blessings Out

Journal

Prayer | Blessings

Blessings Out

Journal

Prayer | Blessings In

Blessings Out

Journal

Prayer | Blessings In

Blessings Out

Journal

Prayer

Blessings
In

Blessings
Out

Journal

Prayer | Blessings In

Blessings Out

Journal

Prayer | Blessings
In

Blessings
Out

Journal

Prayer | Blessings In

Blessings Out

Journal

Prayer | Blessings In

Blessings Out

Journal

Prayer | Blessings In

Blessings Out

Journal

Prayer

Blessings In

Blessings Out

Journal

Prayer | Blessings In

Blessings Out

Journal

Prayer | Blessings
In

Blessings
Out

Journal

Prayer | Blessings In

Blessings Out

Journal

Prayer | Blessings In

Blessings Out

Journal

Prayer | Blessings In

Blessings Out

Journal

Prayer | Blessings
In

Blessings
Out

Journal

Prayer | Blessings In

Blessings Out

Journal

Prayer | Blessings In

Blessings Out

Journal

Prayer | Blessings In

Blessings Out

Journal

Prayer | Blessings
In

Blessings
Out

Journal

Prayer | Blessings In

Blessings Out

Journal

Prayer | Blessings In

Blessings Out

Journal

Prayer

Blessings In

Blessings Out

Journal

Prayer

Blessings In

Blessings Out

Journal

Prayer | Blessings In

Blessings Out

Journal

Prayer | Blessings In

Blessings Out

Journal

Prayer	Blessings In
	Blessings Out

Journal

Prayer | Blessings In

Blessings Out

Journal

Prayer | Blessings In

Blessings Out

Journal

Prayer

Blessings In

Blessings Out

Journal

Prayer | Blessings In

Blessings Out

Journal

Prayer | Blessings In

Blessings Out

Journal

Prayer | Blessings
In

Blessings
Out

Journal

Prayer | Blessings In

Blessings Out

Journal

Prayer | Blessings In

Blessings Out

Journal

Prayer

Blessings
In

Blessings
Out

Journal

Prayer | Blessings In

Blessings Out

Journal

Prayer | Blessings
In

Blessings
Out

Journal

Prayer

Blessings In

Blessings Out

Journal

Prayer | Blessings In

Blessings Out

Journal

Prayer | Blessings In

Blessings Out

Journal

Prayer | Blessings In

Blessings Out

Journal

Prayer | Blessings In

Blessings Out

Journal

Prayer | Blessings In

Blessings Out

Journal

Prayer | Blessings In

Blessings Out

Journal

Prayer

Blessings In

Blessings Out

Journal

Prayer | Blessings In

Blessings Out

Journal

Prayer | Blessings In

Blessings Out

Journal

Prayer | Blessings In

Blessings Out

Journal

Prayer

Blessings
In

Blessings
Out

Journal

Prayer | Blessings In

Blessings Out

Journal

Prayer | Blessings In

Blessings Out

Journal

Prayer | Blessings In

Blessings Out

Journal

Prayer | Blessings In

Blessings Out

Journal

Prayer | Blessings In

Blessings Out

Journal

Prayer | Blessings In

Blessings Out

Journal

Prayer | Blessings In

Blessings Out

Journal

Prayer

Blessings
In

Blessings
Out

Journal

Prayer

Blessings In

Blessings Out

Journal

Prayer | Blessings
In

Blessings
Out

Journal

Prayer | Blessings In

Blessings Out

Journal

Prayer

Blessings
In

Blessings
Out

Journal

Prayer | Blessings In

Blessings Out

Journal

Prayer | Blessings
In

Blessings
Out

Journal

Prayer | Blessings In

Blessings Out

Journal

Prayer | Blessings In

Blessings Out

Journal

Prayer | Blessings In

Blessings Out

Journal

Prayer | Blessings In

Blessings Out

Journal

Prayer | Blessings In

Blessings Out

Journal

Prayer | Blessings In

Blessings Out

Journal

Prayer | Blessings In

Blessings Out

Journal

Prayer | Blessings In
 |
 | Blessings Out

Journal

Prayer | Blessings In
| Blessings Out

Journal

Prayer

Blessings In

Blessings Out

Journal

Prayer

Blessings
In

Blessings
Out

Journal

Prayer

Blessings In

Blessings Out

Journal

Prayer | Blessings In

Blessings Out

Journal

Prayer | Blessings In

Blessings Out

Journal

Prayer | Blessings In

Blessings Out

Journal

Prayer | Blessings
In

Blessings
Out

Journal

Prayer | Blessings In

Blessings Out

Journal

Prayer | Blessings In

Blessings Out

Journal

Prayer | Blessings In

Blessings Out

Journal

Prayer | Blessings In

Blessings Out

Journal

Prayer | Blessings In

Blessings Out

Journal

Prayer | Blessings In

Blessings Out

Journal

Prayer | Blessings In

Blessings Out

Journal

Prayer | Blessings In

Blessings Out

Journal

Prayer | Blessings In

Blessings Out

Journal

Prayer

Blessings In

Blessings Out

Journal

Prayer

Blessings In

Blessings Out

Journal

Prayer

Blessings In

Blessings Out

Journal

Prayer | Blessings In

Blessings Out

Journal

Prayer | Blessings In

Blessings Out

Journal

Prayer | Blessings In

Blessings Out

Journal

Prayer | Blessings In

Blessings Out

Journal

Prayer | Blessings In

Blessings Out

Journal

Prayer | Blessings In

Blessings Out

Journal

Prayer

Blessings In

Blessings Out

Journal

Prayer

Blessings In

Blessings Out

Journal

Prayer

Blessings In

Blessings Out

Journal

Prayer

Blessings In

Blessings Out

Journal

Prayer | Blessings In

Blessings Out

Journal

Prayer | Blessings
In

Blessings
Out

Journal

Prayer

Blessings In

Blessings Out

Journal

Prayer | Blessings In

Blessings Out

Journal

Prayer | Blessings In

Blessings Out

Journal

Prayer | Blessings In

Blessings Out

Journal

Prayer

Blessings
In

Blessings
Out

Journal

Prayer | Blessings In

Blessings Out

Journal

Prayer

Blessings In

Blessings Out

Journal

Prayer | Blessings In

Blessings Out

Journal

Prayer

Blessings In

Blessings Out

Journal

Prayer | Blessings In

Blessings Out

Journal

Prayer

Blessings In

Blessings Out

Journal

Prayer

Blessings In

Blessings Out

Journal

Prayer

Blessings In

Blessings Out

Journal

Prayer | Blessings In

Blessings Out

Journal

Prayer

Blessings
In

Blessings
Out

Journal

Prayer | Blessings
In

| Blessings
Out

Journal

Prayer | Blessings In

Blessings Out

Journal

Prayer | Blessings
In

Blessings
Out

Journal

Prayer | Blessings In

Blessings Out

Journal

Prayer | Blessings In

Blessings Out

Journal

Prayer

Blessings In

Blessings Out

Journal

Prayer | Blessings
In

Blessings
Out

Journal

Prayer | Blessings In

Blessings Out

Journal

Prayer

Blessings
In

Blessings
Out

Made in the USA
Middletown, DE
03 June 2024

55138787R00220